VOYAGES ~OF~ EXPLORATION

Nick Arnold

Wayland

Dangerous Waters

MONSTERS OF THE DEEP
PIRATES AND TREASURE
VOYAGES OF EXPLORATION
THE WHALERS

Fearsome Creatures

BIRDS OF PREY
LAND PREDATORS
NIGHT CREATURES
WHEN DINOSAURS RULED THE
EARTH

Frontiers

JOURNEYS INTO THE UNKNOWN
MAPS AND GLOBES
THE WILD, WILD WEST
THE WORLD'S WILD PLACES

The Earth's Secrets

FOSSILS AND BONES
THE HIDDEN PAST
THE SEARCH FOR RICHES
VOLCANO, EARTHQUAKE AND
FLOOD

Produced by
Roger Coote Publishing, 68 Florence Road
Brighton, East Sussex BN1 6DJ, England

Series designer: Jane Hannath
Book designer: David Armitage

First published in 1995 by
Wayland (Publishers) Limited, 61 Western Road
Hove, East Sussex BN3 1JD, England

© Copyright 1995 Wayland (Publishers) Limited

British Library Cataloguing in Publication Data

Arnold, Nick
    Voyages of Exploration. - (Quest Series)
    I. Title II. Series
    910.9

    ISBN 0 7502 1200 4

Printed and bound in Italy by
G. Canale & C.S.p.A., Turin

Picture acknowledgements
AKG London 1, 5, 9b, 18b, 20b, 24b, 28, 32l, 33b, 34t, 35br, 40t, 45l; Ann Ronan/Image Select 44r; CM Dixon 7tc, 10b, 12t, 16b; ET Archive 11b, 43t; Mary Evans Picture Library 4l, 8t, 11t, 13t, 15t, 17t, 26l, 29b, 30b, 31l, 42; Michael Holford 7b, 9tl, 36b, 37t, 37b, 43b; Peter Newark's Historical Pictures 14tl, 22-23, 27b, 38t, 38-39, 41b; Photri 29t, 41l; Wayland Picture Library 6b, 16l, 22t, 25b, 30t, 33t, 34b, 36r. The artwork is by Barbara Loftus.

CONTENTS

WHY DID PEOPLE EXPLORE?

IMAGINE you are lost in the ocean, with no map and little idea of where you are going. Your ship is leaking badly but there is no chance of repairing it until you find land. There is no fresh food and hardly any water to drink. Some of your crew are sick and dying, and the healthier ones are threatening to throw you overboard. A storm is brewing and the waves are getting higher. You could be shipwrecked, washed up on some desolate shore, or drowned - or swallowed whole by a huge sea monster. You are far from home and there is no one to rescue you. Aren't you sorry you became an explorer?

Many early mariners were terrified that their voyages would take them into regions where the seas were full of monsters like these.

Even in the late eighteenth century, a ship at sea was a very dangerous place and many sailors didn't survive longer than one or two voyages. But the main causes of death were not ship-wrecks or battles with enemy ships. Of every hundred sailors who were killed at sea, 50 died of disease and 32 as a result of accidents.

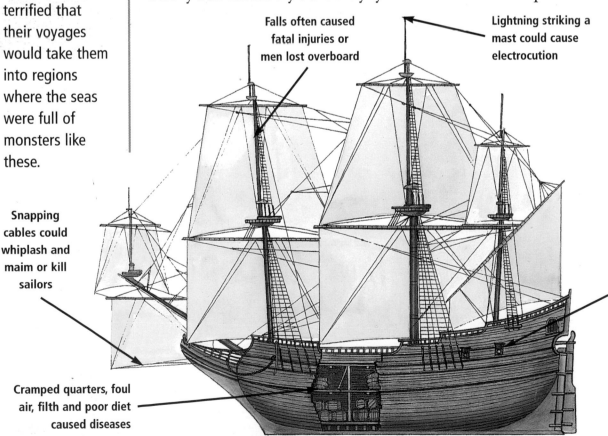

Falls often caused fatal injuries or men lost overboard

Lightning striking a mast could cause electrocution

Snapping cables could whiplash and maim or kill sailors

A gun breaking loose on deck would crush anyone in its path

Cramped quarters, foul air, filth and poor diet caused diseases

Starvation, disease and death

In 1520, the Portuguese mariner Ferdinand Magellan sailed around the tip of South America and into the vast, uncharted Pacific Ocean. He and his men then had to endure 'three months and twenty days without taking in provisions, and we only ate old biscuit reduced to powder, and stinking from the dirt which the rats had made on it ... and we drank water that was yellow and stinking. We also ate the ox hides [strips of leather] which were under the main yard ... also the sawdust of wood, and rats that cost half a ducat each ... and the upper and lower gums of our men grew so much [because of a disease called scurvy] that they could not eat ... and in this way nineteen died ... [and] twenty-five or thirty fell ill'.

The survivors of a shipwreck cling desperately to a section of the mast. They signal in vain to attract the attention of any passing ship - but there are none in sight.

For God, gold and glory

Explorers really did put their lives on the line. But what drove them to face such terrible dangers - to risk their lives in search of the unknown? They all hoped to gain something by exploring. It might be new land, plunder, trade or fame. For some it was a powerful desire to convert others to their religious beliefs. But they all sought to discover more about the world in which they lived, either for themselves or for the benefit of others.

EXPLORERS OF THE ANCIENT WORLD

FROM around 3900 BC, the ancient Egyptians built ships made from bundles of papyrus reeds tied together. They used these simple craft for carrying people and goods along the River Nile.

The first explorers

These early Egyptian shipbuilders also knew how to make stronger ships using wooden planks lashed together with rope. At that time, the only trees in Egypt that could provide timber for shipbuilding were acacia and sycamore, from which only short lengths could be cut. But by 2900 BC, Egyptians were sailing to Byblos in Lebanon to buy cedarwood. Cedar trees grow taller than acacia and sycamore, and so the Egyptians could cut longer planks from them to build larger, ocean-going ships. In these new ships, which carried a single wide sail and were propelled by oars, the Egyptians embarked on long sea voyages for trade and conquest.

Below left In about 1492 BC, Queen Hatshepsut of Egypt sent a trading expedition to the land of Punt. Her sailors travelled in ships like this. Before they could set out, the materials to build the ships had to be hauled 250 km across the desert from the River Nile to the Red Sea, near modern-day Quseir. This was not the first Egyptian expedition to Punt, but it was probably the largest and the most successful.

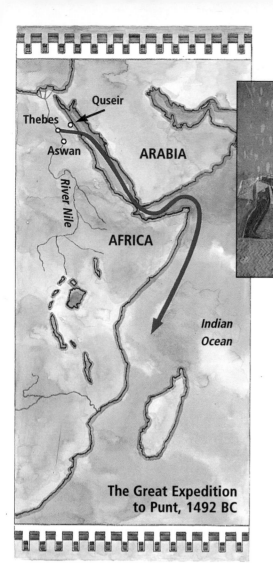

The Great Expedition to Punt, 1492 BC

The Egyptians brought back from Punt ivory, ebony and gold, as well as myrrh and frankincense, which were used for making perfumes. This wall painting shows Egyptians returning from Punt. One of them is carrying a whole myrrh tree for replanting in Egypt.

The Phoenicians

The greatest explorers of ancient times were probably the Phoenicians. They came from a group of city states, including Sidon, Byblos and Tyre, at the eastern end of the Mediterranean Sea in what is now Lebanon, Israel and Syria. They were expert shipbuilders and they became the most powerful merchants in the Mediterranean. By 1000 BC, Phoenician sailors were trading with areas as far away as Spain and Arabia. They founded many trading posts around the shores of the Mediterranean, including Carthage in North Africa, which grew to become very rich and powerful.

The Phoenicians were expert shipbuilders. This relief shows a Phoenician ship of about 700 BC - a bireme with two rows of oars along each side.

On their journey to Punt, Egyptian traders sailed 2,400 km through the shark-infested Red Sea. They then probably headed south down the East Coast of Africa. No one knows exactly where Punt was.

Hanno of Carthage

In the fifth century BC, a nobleman named Hanno led a famous voyage from Carthage. The city rulers had asked him to explore the west coast of Africa and establish new trading settlements there.

Modern scholars believe that Hanno's expedition may have reached Sierra Leone in West Africa. Hanno described seeing animals that were probably elephants and crocodiles in an African river. Unfortunately, the only record we have of Hanno's voyage is one that the Phoenicians wrote to confuse their great trading rivals, the Greeks. They did this to keep their jealously guarded secret - they were trading for gold with the local African people. But their secret must have got

out, because the Greek writer Herodotus was able to describe how they traded.

Herodotus wrote that when sailors from Carthage landed on the West African coast, they spread out their cargo along the water line. They then lit a fire nearby and returned to their ships. 'The people of the country see the smoke and, coming to the sea, they lay down gold to pay for the cargo and withdraw away from the wares. Then the Carthaginians disembark and examine their gold; if it seems to them a fair price for their cargo, they take it and go on their way; but if not, they go aboard again and wait, and then the people come back and add more gold until the ship's crew are satisfied.'

Phoenician trading ships arriving at the port of Alexandria in Egypt

Right The map shows Phoenician and Greek colonies in and around the Mediterranean. From about 3000 BC to 100 BC, the two peoples traded in many goods, including gold and other metals, timber and grain.

Pytheas sails to Thule

The ancient Greeks knew more about the world than any other civilization before them, yet they had no idea what lands might lie beyond the western end of the Mediterranean. Early in the fourth century BC, a Greek astronomer and geographer called Pytheas set sail to find out for himself.

Greek colonies
Phoenician colonies

Atlantic Ocean

GREECE

PHOENICIA

Carthage

NORTH AFRICA

Mediterranean Sea

Colonies in the Mediterranean

A Greek pottery cup dating from about 540 BC. It shows a Greek merchant ship (left) powered by sail, and a warship (right) with both sail and oars. The warship has a bronze spike on its prow, used for ramming and sinking enemy ships.

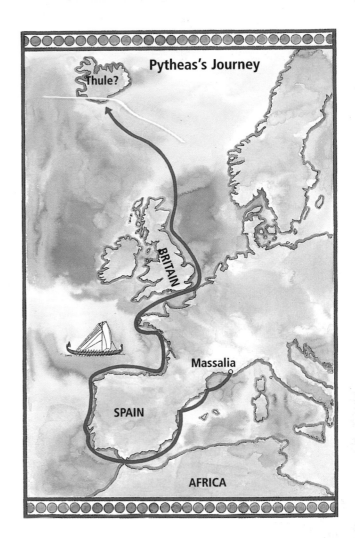

Pytheas's Journey

Pytheas left his home town of Massalia - what is now Marseilles in southern France - and sailed through the Straits of Gibraltar. Turning north, he explored the Atlantic coasts of Portugal, Spain and France, and continued past Britain. Six days after leaving the Scottish coast, Pytheas reached an island he called Thule - possibly modern-day Iceland. Many people have dismissed Pytheas's voyage as fiction, but his story might be true.

The end of an age

When the golden age of Greek civilization ended in the first century BC, it also brought to an end the first great period of exploration by sea. In fact, no new lands across the sea were 'discovered' by European sailors until the time of the Vikings, over 1,300 years after the voyage of Pytheas.

This may have been the route taken by Pytheas on his voyage to Thule in about 310 BC.

Right This map of the world, drawn in about AD 1500, is based on one that was first made by the Greek-Egyptian geographer Ptolemy during the first century AD. Although it shows only Europe, Asia and part of Africa, it was accepted as an accurate view of the world for more than 1,400 years.

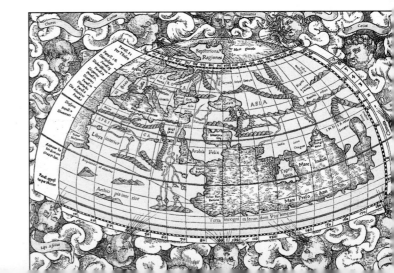

VOYAGES OF THE VIKINGS

IN AD 982, a Viking called Erik the Red quarrelled with his neighbours and killed two of them. At the time, Erik was living in Iceland, where the Vikings had set up a colony about a hundred years earlier. As punishment for his crimes, he was banished for three years and had to make a fast getaway, pursued by the relatives of the men he had murdered.

Erik's trick

Erik sailed west in search of a land which had first been sighted 50 years earlier by a Norwegian named Gunnbjorn. Eventually, Erik found this new land. He called it Greenland, hoping that when his banishment ended and he returned to Iceland, this pleasant-sounding name would help him to tempt people to go and settle there.

Erik's trick worked. In 985 he returned to Greenland with 25 ships crammed with colonists and their animals. Only 14 ships completed the voyage - some of the others turned back to Iceland, but the rest were crushed by huge waves, or 'sea hedges', as the Vikings called them.

Viking warriors struck fear into people's hearts wherever they went. The carved wooden head-posts to their longships must have helped to create fear in those who saw them sailing towards them.

10

When they arrived after their ordeal, the survivors huddled together on the shore, cold and tired, before getting down to the task of building homes for themselves. In all, 190 farmsteads were built around Erik's house at Brattahlid, on Greenland's southwest coast.

Viking warships of about AD 860. At that time, the Vikings were settling in Iceland, England and other countries.

The Viking flood

A bronze weather vane from a Viking ship of the eleventh century

The Vikings came from the lands now known as Norway, Sweden and Denmark. From the eighth to the twelfth century AD, they frequently sailed from their homelands to western Europe and beyond, on voyages of plunder, trade and conquest. In the words of one Irish writer in the ninth century: 'The sea spewed forth floods of foreigners over Erin [Ireland] so that no haven, no landing place, no stronghold, no fort, no castle might be found [that was not] submerged by waves of Vikings and pirates.'

This bronze figure is of the Thor, the Viking god of thunder, storms and sea journeys. It was made in Iceland around AD 1000. Although most Vikings were Christians by that time, Thor was still worshipped by some.

One of the settlers was a man called Herjolf. Shortly after he had left Iceland, his son Bjarni had arrived there. Bjarni was a merchant who traded between Norway and Iceland. When he returned home to Iceland, only to find his father gone, Bjarni decided to follow Herjolf to the new colony in Greenland. But things did not go according to plan.

A missed opportunity

Bjarni's ship was blown south and he and his men lost their way. Eventually they sighted a country of low, wooded hills. The exhausted crew thought this would be good place to rest but Bjarni refused to land. The shore didn't look anything like the description he had been given of Greenland, and Bjarni wanted to find his father as soon as possible. And so, at that moment, Bjarni Herjolfsson may have missed his chance to become the first European to land in America.

A Viking long-ship could be over 30 m long and about 5 or 6 m wide, and could carry up to 80 warriors.

Single large sail used at sea, when winds favourable

Only shelter on board - hut for helmsman

Steering oar

Carved prow in form of real or mythical creature

Oars used when there was no wind, or if wind in wrong direction

Bjarni turned north and found two more lands. One was wooded and the other bleak and mountainous. Scholars think that he probably glimpsed the coasts of Labrador and Baffin Island, in what is now northeast Canada. At last, a gale blew the ship back to Greenland and Bjarni was reunited with his father. Glad to have survived, he settled down at Herjolf's farm and never went exploring again.

A Viking ship off the coast of Markland. This was the name given by Leif Eriksson to what is now Labrador.

Leif's voyage to America

According to Viking legend, Bjarni's voyage caused 'great talk of discovering new countries.' At their farmstead in Brattahlid, Erik the Red and his son Leif made plans to explore the new lands. Leif visited Bjarni and bought his ship from him. In about AD 1000, he put to sea with a crew of 35 men to find the lands that Bjarni had described. After landing on Baffin Island and on the coast of Labrador, they sailed on and found what they took to be the mainland.

Above The main sea routes of the Vikings, including what they called the 'Western Way' from Norway to Iceland, Greenland and on to North America.

Left Leif Eriksson strides ashore on the coast of Vinland in about AD 1000.

Tyrkir and the vines

One Viking legend, written down in what are called The Vinland Sagas, tells how this new land got its name - Vinland.

'One evening news came that someone was missing: it was Tyrkir the Southerner ... Leif got ready to make a search with twelve men.

'They had gone only a short distance ... when Tyrkir came towards them. He said, "I have some news. I found vines and grapes."

'Next morning Leif said to his men, "Now we have two tasks on our hands ... we must gather grapes and cut vines, and then fell trees to make a cargo for my ship."

'This was done. It is said that the tow-boat was filled with grapes. They took on a full cargo of timber; and in the spring ... they sailed away [back to Greenland]. Leif named the country ... Vinland.'

Who discovered America?

The first people to arrive in North America were the native Americans. They walked from Asia to Alaska more than 30,000 years ago, when the sea-level was lower than it is today and Siberia and Alaska were joined together by a so-called 'land-bridge'.

It is possible that the Vikings may not have been the first Europeans to reach America - the Irish monk Saint Brendan may have got there 500 years before them. The monks certainly sailed to the Faeroe Islands and Iceland in their small leather boats, called curraghs. According to legend, they also reached an island which may have been Newfoundland. In the 1970s, Tim Severin set out in a similar craft to prove that such a journey was possible. He sailed his curragh through gales and thick fog from Ireland to the Faeroes, Iceland, Greenland and on to Labrador in North America.

There is a legend that Saint Brendan landed on the back of a whale, thinking it was an island.

Leif and his men went ashore and built huts for shelter. Nearby they found streams full of the largest salmon they had ever seen.

The Skraelings

In about AD 1004, Leif's brother Thorwald sailed to Vinland with 30 men. They spent the winter in Leif's huts before exploring further along the coast. One day in the summer of 1005, Thorwald and his men came across nine native Americans, whom they called 'Skraelings'. They may have been American Indians or Inuits. Whoever they were, the Vikings killed eight of them but the ninth escaped. The next day the Vikings were attacked by a large native war party, and Thorwald was killed.

PIONEERS OF THE SPICE ROUTE

FOLLOWING the decline of the Vikings' civilization, there was a period in which European exploration by sea came almost to a complete halt. But then, in the fifteenth century, the Portuguese set in motion the next great age of exploration. They set sail in search of the fabulous riches of the Far East: silk, pearls and - most valuable of all - spices.

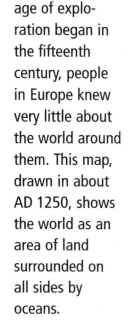

Before the great age of exploration began in the fifteenth century, people in Europe knew very little about the world around them. This map, drawn in about AD 1250, shows the world as an area of land surrounded on all sides by oceans.

Arab traders in the Indian Ocean

For centuries, spices had been brought to Europe by Arab merchants, who sailed in vessels called dhows, which had pointed ends and triangular, or lateen, sails. The dhow captains were skilled navigators. Like the ancient Greeks, they used the astrolabe to help them find their way. Even more useful at sea was the kamal - a simple device for measuring the height of the pole star above the horizon in order to calculate latitude.

The astrolabe was invented by the Arab astronomers in about AD 700. It was used to find out the height of the sun and stars above the horizon, which enabled people to calculate their latitude. A special version of the astrolabe was invented for use on ships at sea.

The spice trade

Today you can buy cloves, cinnamon, pepper, nutmeg and other spices in almost any supermarket. But in fifteenth-century Europe, they were fabulously expensive, and were worth more than their weight in gold.

These spices were grown in India, Sri Lanka and the so-called Spice Islands - part of modern-day Indonesia - and were in great demand in Europe for flavouring food. The overland journey from the East to Europe was long and hazardous, with many bandits lying in wait to attack unwary travellers. The sea routes across the Indian Ocean were controlled by Arab traders, who bought the spices in the East and sold them to merchants from the Italian cities of Venice and Genoa. The Venetian and Genoese merchants then sold them in Europe, charging about a hundred times as much as the spices had cost in the East.

Merchants from the city of Venice buying goods from Arab traders in about 1400.

The Arabs also learnt to use the seasonal monsoon winds that blow across the Indian Ocean. The summer monsoon blew their ships northeastwards from their trading posts on the East African coast to the ports of India, while the winter monsoon drove them back across the ocean.

Right The Arabs were not the only people sailing the Indian Ocean in the fifteenth century. For centuries, Chinese sailors and merchants had been trading with East Africa. In 1405 a vast fleet set out from China to explore the Indian Ocean. Its commander was Cheng Ho, a high-ranking soldier in the service of the Chinese Emperor Cheng Tsu.

Cheng Ho led a further six expeditions, visiting Thailand, India, Arabia and the East Indies. He may even have sailed round the southern tip of Africa into the Atlantic Ocean as early as 1420.

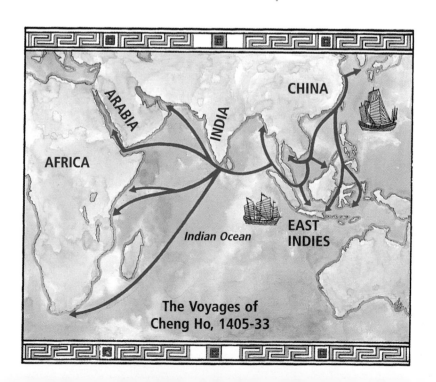

The Voyages of Cheng Ho, 1405-33

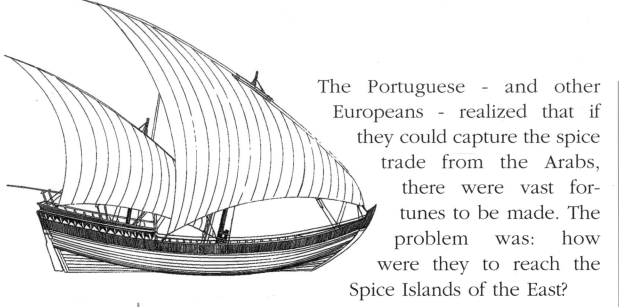

The Portuguese - and other Europeans - realized that if they could capture the spice trade from the Arabs, there were vast fortunes to be made. The problem was: how were they to reach the Spice Islands of the East?

Dhows like this have been used by Arab traders for centuries.

South to the Cape

In 1487, Bartholomew Diaz set out from Portugal to sail as far as he could down the African coast. His fleet consisted of two ships and a supply vessel stocked with extra provisions.

A tremendous storm blew up, and for 13 days his small ships were driven south out of sight of land.

Prince Henry's quest

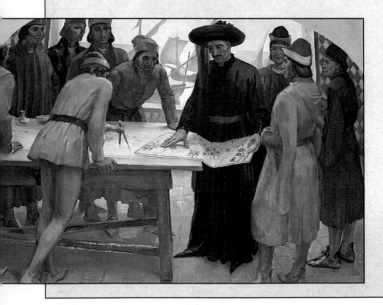

Prince Henry planning voyages with his sea captains

In 1419 Prince Henry - son of the Portuguese King John I - set up a school of navigation in an old fort on the rocky shores of the bay of Sagres. He believed that there were rich trading opportunities to be had along the northwest coast of Africa, and began sending out expeditions to explore and report back.

According to his friend Gomez Eannes de Azurara, Henry wanted: 'To discover what lay beyond the Canaries and Cape Bojador; to trade with any Christians who might dwell in the lands beyond; to discover the extent of the Muslim dominions; to spread the

When he finally saw land again, Diaz realized that the coast stretched away to the northeast. He was certain that he had found the east coast of Africa, and that India and the Spice Islands lay beyond. Diaz wanted to go on, but his crew mutinied and forced him to turn back. The exhausted men were terrified that if they went too far they would lose contact with their supply vessel and starve to death.

The cross-staff (top) was used to work out the height of the North Star above the horizon. The lower it was in the sky, the further south was the ship. The mariner's astrolabe (left) was also used for calculating latitude from the positions of stars.

Christian faith; to fulfil the predictions of his horoscope, which bound him to engage in great and noble conquests and attempt the discovery of things that were hidden from other men.'

Year after year, Henry urged his captains to explore further southwards. By the time he died in 1460, his ships had sailed as far south as modern-day Sierra Leone in West Africa. The merchant voyages continued after his death, paid for by a growing trade in gold, ivory and slaves.

In 1487, the Portuguese explorer Bartholomew Diaz succeeded in sailing round the tip of Africa and into the Indian Ocean.

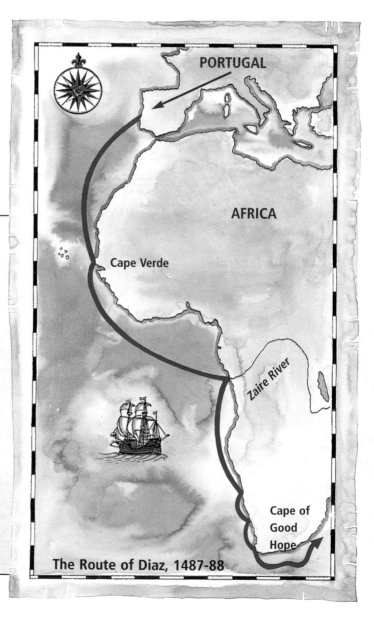

PORTUGAL

AFRICA

Cape Verde

Zaire River

Cape of Good Hope

The Route of Diaz, 1487-88

On the return voyage Diaz saw a point that he had missed on his gale-tossed outward voyage. He christened it the 'Cape of Storms', but John II of Portugal re-named it the 'Cape of Good Hope'. He had reason to be hopeful: the Portuguese now had a chance to sail round Africa to Asia and cash in on the profitable spice trade.

In search of spices

On 8 July 1497, a fleet of four Portuguese ships led by Vasco da Gama left the port of Lisbon and headed for the open sea. His orders from King Manuel I were to '… make discoveries and go in search of spices'.

Da Gama steered far west of the direct course down the African coast. He was trying to avoid the northerly coastal current and pick up westerly winds to take him round the Cape of Good Hope. But his progress was very slow, and food and fresh water ran low. The men were forced to cook what little food they had in sea water. On 22 November, the Portuguese ships rounded the Cape and headed up the east coast of Africa.

Vasco da Gama. During his first voyage to India, many of his men died of disease, and only 55 of the original 170 made it back to Portugal.

A caravel of the fifteenth century. It was in ships like this that many of the early Portuguese mariners set sail. They had lateen sails - similar to those of Arab dhows - and a shallow draught that enabled them to explore shallow coastal waters.

A party at Mossel Bay

On 2 December 1497, da Gama and his men landed at Mossel Bay, just beyond the Cape of Good Hope, where they were welcomed by the local inhabitants. 'On Saturday, about 200 Negroes came, both young and old. They brought with them about a dozen oxen and cows and four or five sheep. As soon as we saw them we went ashore. They ... began to play on four or five flutes, some producing high notes and others low ones, thus making a pretty harmony ... and they danced ... The Captain Major [da Gama] then ordered the trumpets to be sounded, and we in the boats danced, and the Captain Major did so likewise when he rejoined us. This festivity ended, we ... bought a black ox for three bracelets. This ox we dined off on Sunday. We found him very fat and toothsome [tasty] as the beef of Portugal.'

Into the Arab world

As he sailed north, da Gama entered regions where the Arabs had great influence, especially over trade. The Sultan of Mozambique welcomed the Portuguese at first, because he thought they were Muslims - either Moors from North Africa or Turks - and he went aboard da Gama's ship to dine with them. But when he discovered that they were Christians, he refused to trade with them, and treated the goods they had brought with contempt.

The spread of Islam

Islam was founded by the prophet Muhammad (c. AD 570-632) in about AD 600, and it spread very quickly throughout the Middle East, North Africa and beyond.

Vasco da Gama found that most of the countries he visited in East Africa were Muslim. That was because the Islamic religion had been taken there by Arab traders.

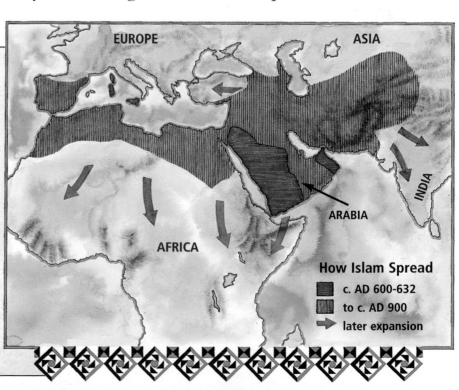

EUROPE
ASIA
INDIA
ARABIA
AFRICA

How Islam Spread
- c. AD 600-632
- to c. AD 900
- later expansion

The traverse board was used along with a compass to help the helmsman to keep track of the course he was sailing. Every half-hour (measured by the hour-glass) the pegs were moved in the direction of the ship's course.

Relations between the explorers and the local people grew worse. When a group of armed men tried to prevent the Portuguese from going ashore for fresh water, da Gama fired on them with a cannon. News of this attack travelled up the coast and guaranteed the explorers a hostile welcome when they reached Mombasa, in what is now Kenya.

The Sultan of Mombasa promised the Portuguese that they would be safe if they went ashore, but da Gama feared a trap. To get at the truth, he tortured two Muslim captives by dropping boiling oil on their skin. The men told him that the explorers would be seized if they landed, and punished for their behaviour in Mozambique. That night, two boatloads of armed men came to attack the Portuguese ships, and swimmers tried to cut their anchor cables. Da Gama's ships had to leave in a hurry.

They sailed on to Malindi where, fortunately, the sultan proved friendlier and presented the explorers with fresh food and spices. One of the sailors wrote that 'The King [sultan] wore a robe of damask trimmed with green satin … He was seated on two cushioned chairs of bronze, beneath a round sunshade of crimson satin … An old man

The East African port of Zanzibar in 1878. Almost 400 years after da Gama's voyage, Arab traders were still present there, as we can see by the two dhows lying offshore. On the left of the picture is a European sailing ship.

who attended him as a page carried a short sword in a silver sheath. There were many players on anafils, and two trumpets of ivory, richly carved and the size of a man'. The Sultan of Malindi also supplied a pilot who could guide da Gama's fleet to their final destination, across the ocean to India.

Vasco da Gama's route in 1497-99. His outward course took him far into the Atlantic. This helped him to avoid both the doldrums - an area where sailing ships can be held up by lack of wind - and the strong Guinea Current which flows northward along the African coast. This course was followed by other sailing ships in later centuries.

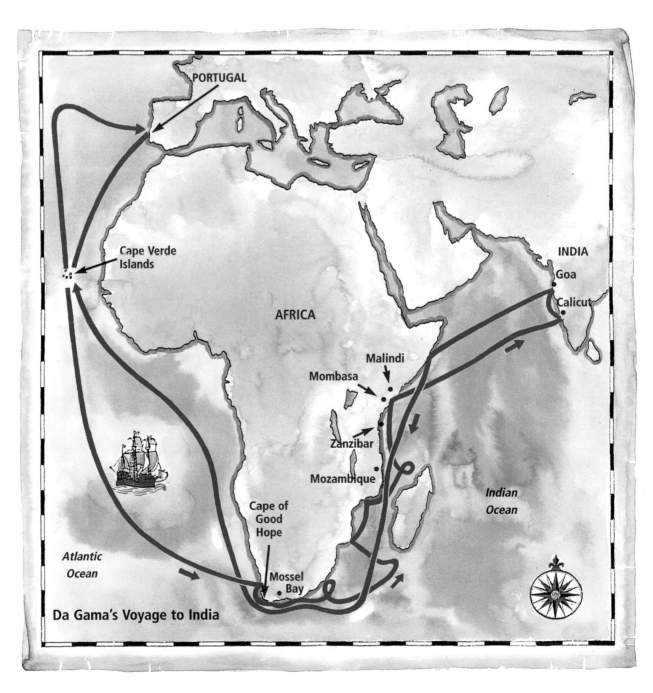

PORTUGAL

Cape Verde Islands

INDIA
Goa
Calicut

AFRICA

Malindi
Mombasa
Zanzibar
Mozambique

Indian Ocean

Cape of Good Hope

Atlantic Ocean

Mossel Bay

Da Gama's Voyage to India

Da Gama and his men buying goods from traders in Calicut

Calicut

The fleet reached the Indian city of Calicut on 20 May 1498. Da Gama had great hopes of trading for spices and jewels, but the Zamorin - the local king - rejected the cheap goods offered by the Portuguese. The trade in Calicut was controlled by Arab merchants, and they did everything they could to prevent the explorers from taking any of it away from them. Eventually, da Gama and his men managed to buy a small quantity of jewels and spices in a local market. By then, the Indians and the Portuguese had come to distrust each other thoroughly, and da Gama decided to head for home. In September 1499, the two remaining ships of the fleet reached Lisbon in Portugal.

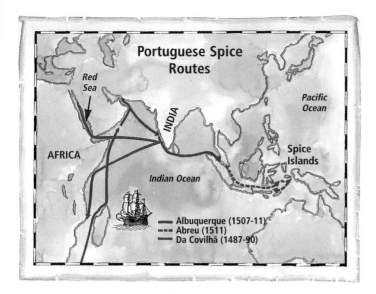

Portuguese Spice Routes

Red Sea
Pacific Ocean
INDIA
AFRICA
Spice Islands
Indian Ocean

— Albuquerque (1507-11)
--- Abreu (1511)
— Da Covilhã (1487-90)

Return to India

Although his voyage was not a great success in terms of trade, Vasco da Gama had proved that it was possible to sail around Africa to India. King Manuel was clearly very pleased - in 1500 he gave himself the title of 'Lord of the Conquest, Navigation and Commerce of India, Arabia and Persia'.

Two years later, da Gama returned to India with a large armed fleet, and managed to seize control of the spice trade from the Arabs. By the time he died in 1524, the Portuguese had crushed the East African sultanates and built up their own trading empire. As a result, Portugal became one of the richest nations in Europe.

Left The first Portuguese sailor to reach India was Pedro da Covilhã in 1487. He sailed through the Mediterranean and down the Red Sea. After da Gama's expedition of 1498-99, the route from India to the Spice Islands was opened up by Afonso de Albuquerque and António de Abreu.

Scurvy - the scourge of the seas

Scurvy was a horrible disease that killed thousands of sailors on long voyages of discovery. It caused a victim's gums to bleed and swell up, making it impossible to eat. The teeth came loose and fell out, the arms and legs became stiff and painful, and sores erupted on the skin.

Scurvy was a serious problem in da Gama's time, and continued until the middle of the eighteenth century - even though a cure had been discovered as early as 1605 when a sea captain cured an outbreak by giving his men lemon juice to drink. This cure worked because the disease is actually caused by a lack of vitamin C, *which is found in fresh fruit and vegetables. Sadly, this information did not reach most ordinary sailors, who continued to die a painful, unnecessary death.*

The real breakthrough came in 1757, when a Royal Navy physician called Dr James Lind published his Treatise on Scurvy, *in which he recommended eating fresh fruit and vegetables to prevent the disease.*

A ship's cook of the eighteenth century

SAILING WEST TO REACH THE EAST

Christopher Columbus. This portrait was painted some time after Columbus's death, and no one is sure exactly what the explorer really looked like.

CHRISTOPHER Columbus was born in Genoa, Italy, in about 1451. From an early age he studied navigation and, like most educated people, he knew the Earth was round. But he also believed the world to be much smaller than it really is.

In the late 1470s, when he was living and working in Portugal, he calculated that the islands of Japan, at the edge of Asia, were less than 4,000 km to the west of Europe. Columbus was a highly experienced sailor and he knew that a voyage of almost 4,000 km would be dangerous - but it could be done. What he didn't know was that Japan is a lot further away than he thought - over 17,000 km.

Rejection and despair

Columbus did not have enough money to pay for such a voyage, and so he spent 13 years badgering the rulers of Portugal and Spain to support him. First he tried John II of Portugal, but the king's advisors told him that Columbus was wrong about the size of the Earth. Columbus then presented his plan to King Ferdinand and Queen Isabella of Spain.

After years of delay, Spanish experts came to the same conclusion as those in Portugal - Columbus had got his sums wrong. In January 1492 he was close to despair, and he set off for France, in search of funds. But as he reached the bridge at Pinos he heard hoofbeats behind him. It was a royal messenger with important news: Ferdinand and Isabella had decided to pay for his venture.

Columbus says farewell to Ferdinand and Isabella before setting out on his first voyage to the New World.

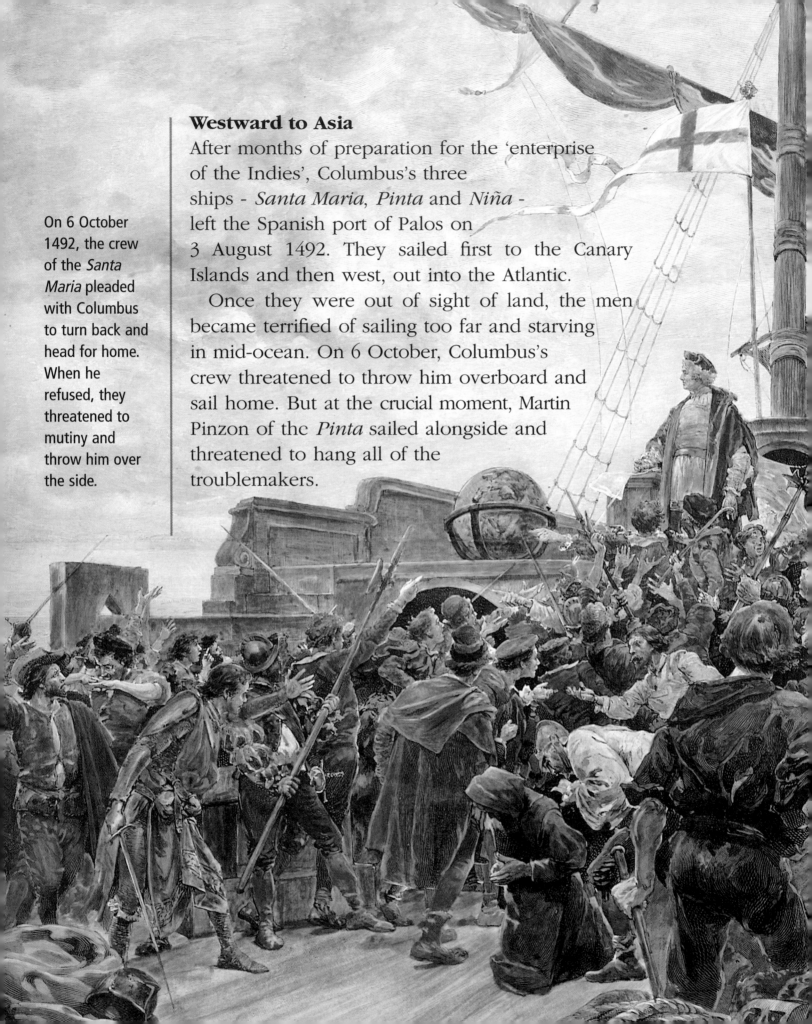

Westward to Asia

After months of preparation for the 'enterprise of the Indies', Columbus's three ships - *Santa Maria*, *Pinta* and *Niña* - left the Spanish port of Palos on 3 August 1492. They sailed first to the Canary Islands and then west, out into the Atlantic.

Once they were out of sight of land, the men became terrified of sailing too far and starving in mid-ocean. On 6 October, Columbus's crew threatened to throw him overboard and sail home. But at the crucial moment, Martin Pinzon of the *Pinta* sailed alongside and threatened to hang all of the troublemakers.

On 6 October 1492, the crew of the *Santa Maria* pleaded with Columbus to turn back and head for home. When he refused, they threatened to mutiny and throw him over the side.

Landfall in the New World

Soon the men were heartened by sightings of birds and driftwood which suggested that land was near. At midnight on 11 October, Columbus stood on the deck of his ship, the *Santa Maria*, and stared into the darkness. He thought he could make out a faint light ahead that looked rather like a small candle. At 2 am the look-out aboard the *Pinta* raised the cry of 'land'. The next day Columbus went ashore. He called the new land San Salvador, meaning 'holy saviour'.

Columbus lands on San Salvador. It is now called Watling Island and is part of the Bahamas.

Trading with the Indians

On his return to Spain in 1493, Columbus wrote a report on his voyage for Ferdinand and Isabella. In it he described the so-called 'Indians' he had met on San Salvador. '... they are so free with all they possess, that no one would believe it without having seen it. Of anything they have, if you ask them for it they never say no; rather they invite the person to share it, and ... are content with whatever little thing ... may be given to them. I forbade that they should be given things so worthless as pieces of broken crockery and broken glass, and ends of straps, though when they were able to get them they thought they had the best jewel in the world; thus it was ascertained that a sailor received for a strap gold to the weight of two and a half castellanos ... They believe very firmly that I, with these ships and people, came from the sky ... and this does not result from their being ignorant, for they are of a very keen intelligence and men who navigate all those seas.'

Columbus and his men trading with the inhabitants they found on San Salvador

An hour-glass was used to keep time. It took one hour for all the sand to run from the top container into the bottom one. As soon as it had finished, the hour-glass was turned upside-down.

The explorers continued on their search for Japan and China. They landed on the Caribbean island of Cuba, which Columbus thought was the southeast corner of China, and then sailed on to Hispaniola (now Haiti and the Dominican Republic). On Christmas eve 1492, Columbus fell into bed, exhausted by lack of sleep. The helmsman of the *Santa Maria* was also weary and he went to sleep leaving a young boy to hold the heavy tiller that steered the ship. As the boy turned the hour-glass to mark the passing time, the *Santa Maria* suddenly shuddered to a halt: it had hit a sand-bank. Columbus had to abandon his ship and return to Spain on the *Niña*.

Heading into trouble

Soon Columbus was on his way back across the Atlantic with a larger fleet. His orders were to settle Hispaniola, explore Cuba and make sure that the Portuguese did not interfere in Spain's new territories. He visited Dominica, Guadeloupe, Puerto Rico and Jamaica, and set up the first European town in the New World - Isabella, on the north coast of Hispaniola.

On his return to Spain, Columbus was summoned to the court of Ferdinand and Isabella. He took gifts of gold and amber, green and yellow parrots, and people from the lands he had visited.

The world divided

The discoveries made by Columbus during his first voyage caused great ill-feeling between Spain and Portugal. In 1494, after two years of wrangling, they agreed to divide the world in two with an imaginary boundary drawn down the middle of the Atlantic Ocean. Lands discovered to the west of the line - such as South America - would belong to Spain, while those of the east - including Africa - would be Portuguese.

But the dividing line ran through Brazil in South America. When Pedro Alvarez Cabral accidentally reached the Brazilian coast in 1500, he claimed it for Portugal. That is why people in Brazil still speak Portuguese while all the other countries of South America have Spanish as their main language.

However, things did not go well. Columbus was a better seaman than a governor, and he quarrelled bitterly with the Spanish colonists he had brought on the voyage. Far less gold was found than people had expected, and the royal court sent an official to report. Columbus returned to Spain, humiliated.

Above On his second expedition, Columbus went in search of gold, but he found very little.

Right Columbus made four journeys to the New World. He was sure that he was only a short distance from China and Japan.

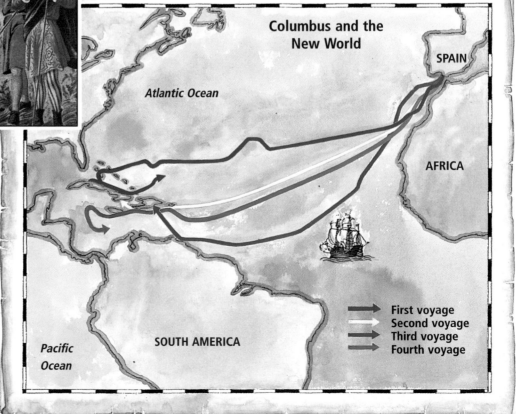

Columbus and the New World

SPAIN

Atlantic Ocean

AFRICA

SOUTH AMERICA

Pacific Ocean

➤ First voyage
➤ Second voyage
➤ Third voyage
➤ Fourth voyage

The bitter end

Columbus managed to get back into the king and queen's good books, and in 1498 he set sail again. This time he reached Trinidad and then landed on the mainland of South America, in what is now Venezuela. But news of more unrest on Hispaniola forced Ferdinand and Isabella to send a new governor to take charge of the colony. This official arrested Columbus and sent him back to Spain in chains.

The explorer never recovered from his hurt and bitterness. 'I was treated as if I had stolen the Indies,' he complained. He even kept the chains in his room as a reminder of his humiliation. Columbus died in 1506, two years after a final unsuccessful voyage in search of Asia.

Ferdinand Magellan

Magellan was a fine navigator and seaman who had taken part in several Portuguese expeditions to India and the Spice Islands during the early years of the sixteenth century. When he returned to Portugal, he heard reports that some Portuguese sailors had found a channel that led from the Atlantic around the southern tip of South America. Magellan was certain that he could sail through this channel and on to the Spice Islands, but he could not persuade King Manuel I of Portugal to give him command of an expedition to prove it. So, like Columbus before him, he took his plans across the border to Spain.

In this painting, Magellan is portrayed navigating his way through all kinds of dangers, with the help of a protecting angel.

The Spanish had not forgotten Columbus's dream of reaching Asia by sailing west. Magellan soon found financiers to back him and then presented his plans to the Spanish king, Charles I. Charles was suspicious at first, but the prospect of cashing in on the spice trade helped him overcome his doubts. On 20 September 1519, Magellan set sail with a fleet of five ships. His orders were to sail to the Spice Islands and on to the Philippines.

Mutiny and shipwreck

After crossing the Atlantic, the expedition sailed down the South American coast. They hunted in vain for the passage around the tip of the continent, before wintering for five months in the bleak bay of San Julian on the barren coast of Patagonia.

Discontent grew while they were there. On 1 April 1520 mutineers seized three of Magellan's five ships. But Magellan fought back. One of his loyal ships blocked the harbour entrance and there was a short but bloody fight. When Magellan regained control, he had one of the ringleaders beheaded and the body of another chopped into pieces.

A sixteenth-century carrack, with a square sail on the main mast and a lateen sail on the third, or mizzen, mast. It was in ships like this that Magellan's expedition set out on what was to be the first voyage around the world.

AMERICUS VESPUTIUS

Amerigo Vespucci

Other Europeans reached the Americas at around the same time as Columbus. Amerigo Vespucci (left) claimed that between 1499 and 1504 he went on several voyages to North and South America, but historians are not sure if this is truth. Nonetheless, he was certain that what Columbus had found was a new continent, and not part of Asia. In 1507 a German mapmaker suggested naming it America, after Amerigo Vespucci.

Magellan directs his fleet from a small boat as the ships pick their way through the passage from the Atlantic to the Pacific. It took the expedition 5 weeks to find a route through the winding strait that was later named after Magellan.

Off one of the Marianas Islands in the Pacific, two of Magellan's men try out a local sailing boat. The picture is from an account of the voyage by António Pigafetta, who sailed with Magellan.

Another mutineer was abandoned on the barren shore with no hope of rescue. To add to Magellan's problems, one of his ships was wrecked in storms while probing further down the coast.

Into the Pacific

On 23 August 1520, Magellan set out again on his southward course. Two months later, his men finally discovered a narrow strait at the tip of South America, leading to the Pacific Ocean. The crew aboard one of Magellan's ships then mutinied and left for home, exhausted by the struggle through this treacherous sea corridor.

The remaining three ships of the fleet carried on, entering the Pacific on 27 November 1520. Magellan felt sure that he was only a few days' sailing from the Spice Islands. But he had not bargained for the vastness of the Pacific. As days turned into weeks and months, and no land was sighted, food and water ran low and many men died of scurvy.

At last, on 28 March 1521, the ships reached the Philippines. Magellan befriended a local Rajah and converted him to Christianity. But then Magellan rashly offered to attack some enemies of his new ally on a neighbouring island. The explorers were beaten back and Magellan was killed in the retreat.

The first voyage around the world

The survivors reached the Spice Islands on 8 November 1521. Only two ships now remained and one of them, the *Victoria*, was seaworthy. Captained by Sebastian del Cano, it headed back for Spain via the Cape of Good Hope.

Again food ran low and there was nothing to eat except rice. More men died of scurvy. At last, on 6 September 1522, the *Victoria* reached Seville in Spain. Of the 277 seafarers who had set out almost three years earlier, only 18 remained alive. They were the first men to sail around the world.

The route sailed by Magellan from Spain to the Philippines, and the return journey of the *Victoria* under Sebastian del Cano.

The tiny *Victoria* - the first ship ever to sail around the world.

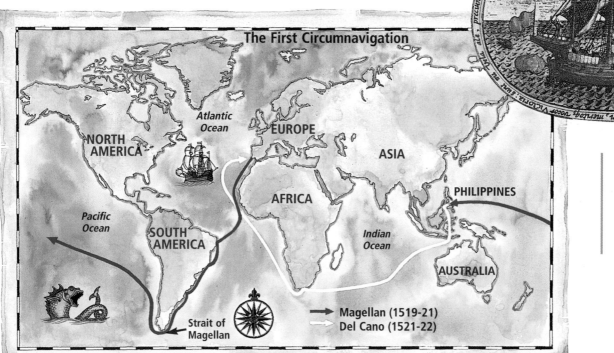

The First Circumnavigation

NORTH AMERICA

Atlantic Ocean

EUROPE

ASIA

AFRICA

PHILIPPINES

Pacific Ocean

SOUTH AMERICA

Indian Ocean

AUSTRALIA

Strait of Magellan

→ Magellan (1519-21)
→ Del Cano (1521-22)

EXPLORING THE SOUTH SEAS

JAMES Cook was born in a village in the north of England in 1728. His parents apprenticed him to a shopkeeper, but the young man was determined to become a seafarer. He spent 10 years learning navigation in the coal-shipping business. He might have made a successful ship's master but in 1755 he volunteered for the Royal Navy. It was a brave decision. At that time the navy had to kidnap men and force them to serve on its ships because the conditions were so appalling that countless seamen died from accident or disease.

Cook proved himself to be an outstanding navigator. In 1759 he piloted an expedition led by General Wolfe up the treacherous St Lawrence River in Canada. The expedition captured the French city of Quebec and won Canada for the British Empire. Cook spent the next eight years charting the Canadian coast.

A Royal Navy sailor of the eighteenth century. Life at sea was dangerous, and few men volunteered to join the Navy. Many sailors had been kidnapped by 'press-gangs'.

James Cook's early days at sea were spent transporting coal down the East coast of England in coal ships known as Whitby cats.

In search of Terra Australis

In 1768 the Admiralty ordered Cook to take a scientific expedition to the South Pacific island of Tahiti. There they planned to observe the passage of the planet Venus across the sun.

These Tahitian war canoes were painted by William Hodges, who sailed with Cook.

Terra Australis

Terra Australis is Latin for 'southern land'. For centuries, geographers and map-makers had been convinced that, in the far south of the world, there must be a huge, unknown continent. They thought that it had to be there in order to balance out the weight of all the known lands in the northern part of the world.

In the years leading up to Cook's voyage, some people thought that New Zealand - sighted in 1642 by the Dutch seaman Abel Tasman - and the north and west coasts of Australia might form part of this mysterious continent.

This Dutch map of about 1570 shows a vast continent at the south of the world. It is marked *Terra Australis Nondum Cognita*, meaning 'southern land not yet discovered. The map-maker was clearly convinced that it would in time be found.

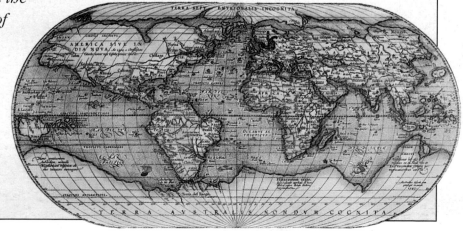

Cook lands at Botany Bay on the east coast of Australia. In this painting, he is shown telling his men not to kill the two Aborigines who are attacking them.

Cook left England at the end of August 1768 aboard the ship *Endeavour*, and reached Tahiti on 11 April 1769, in good time for the scientists to witness the transit of Venus. Then he opened secret orders directing him to find 'Terra Australis', a vast undiscovered continent which many people believed lay in the world's southern oceans.

Cook charted the coasts of New Zealand and then headed for Australia, where he landed at Botany Bay on 28 April 1770. The name reflects the many previously unknown plants collected by the expedition's botanist. Two Aborigines attacked the Europeans, firing darts at them, but Cook frightened them off by firing muskets into the air.

After exploring up the east coast, Cook sailed around the north of Australia to Batavia (now Jakarta in Indonesia) and on to England. He returned home on 13 July 1771 after a voyage of almost three years.

Cook's last voyage

He reached England in 1775, but found it difficult to settle into a shore-based job. In 1776 he volunteered to lead an expedition to find a Northwest Passage linking the Atlantic and Pacific Oceans to the north of Canada. Once again Cook visited New

While the *Endeavour* was exploring up the Australian coast, it struck the Great Barrier Reef and was holed. The ship had to be hauled on to its side to be patched up. The repair work took 2 months.

The icy Antarctic

In 1772, Cook led another expedition in search of Terra Australis. This time, he was to look further south. He actually sailed all the way around the frozen continent of Antarctica, although he never got close enough to see it. No previous explorer had ventured so far south. In the stormy Antarctic Ocean, the seafarers' hands froze to the rigging. Cook's progress was halted by pack ice, and so he headed for home, certain that Terra Australis was a myth.

Zealand and Tahiti. He then sailed north, reaching the Hawaiian Islands in January 1778. Pushing northward again, he passed Vancouver Island, off the west coast of Canada, and entered the Bering Strait. On 18 August, pack ice prevented him from sailing his ship, *Resolution*, any further north, and so he returned south to Hawaii.

When he arrived there, the people welcomed him as a god. They believed he was a divine chieftain called Lono, who had left the island long ago, saying that he would return in a great ship, bringing many gifts.

The expedition stayed in Hawaii for almost three months. It was there, on 14 February 1779, that Cook met his death in a fight with local people.

Cook was a remarkable navigator and he charted coasts he visited with great accuracy. These are the routes of his three epic voyages.

The death of Cook. He and his men had outstayed their welcome in Hawaii, and when a quarrel broke out, it led to a fight in which Cook was killed.

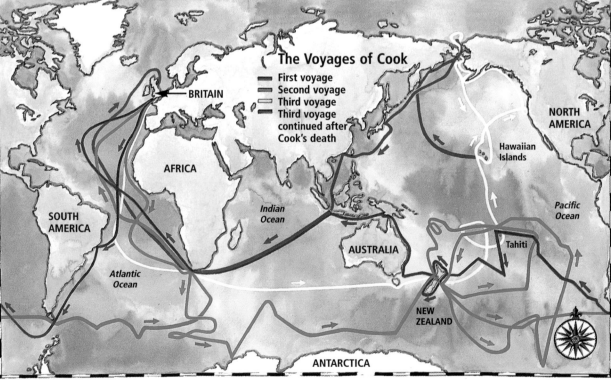

The Voyages of Cook
- First voyage
- Second voyage
- Third voyage
- Third voyage continued after Cook's death

BRITAIN

NORTH AMERICA

AFRICA

Hawaiian Islands

Indian Ocean

Pacific Ocean

SOUTH AMERICA

AUSTRALIA

Tahiti

Atlantic Ocean

NEW ZEALAND

ANTARCTICA

ACROSS THE TOP OF THE WORLD

IN about 1500, European sailors began searching for a sea passage through the Arctic to Asia, around the north of Canada. By that time, the Spanish and Portuguese dominated the trade routes to the East via the southern oceans, and other European countries were forced to look for routes to the north.

Henry Hudson

One of the most famous explorers who searched for the Northwest Passage was Henry Hudson, who led four Arctic expeditions in the early seventeenth century. On his fourth voyage, in 1610, Hudson explored Hudson Bay (which was named after him) in northern Canada. He was certain that he had discovered the fabled sea passage to Asia. But he was tragically mistaken.

As winter came on, Hudson's little ship Discovery *was trapped in the ice. Supplies ran low during the long, dark winter and the cold, hungry crew accused Hudson of hoarding food. In June 1611 the ice melted and Hudson announced that the search would continue. But his men had had enough. They bundled Hudson, his teenage son and seven sick crewmen into a small rowing boat. Then they set the boat adrift. Hudson and his party were never seen again.*

This painting, called *The Last Voyage of Henry Hudson*, shows the explorer, his son and one of his sick crewmen after they had been cast adrift by mutineers. None of them survived.

The Franklin expedition

In May 1845, Sir John Franklin led a well-equipped British expedition in search of the Northwest Passage. Franklin was an elderly but experienced explorer who was well liked by his men. His two ships, *Erebus* and *Terror*, had iron prows to protect them from the ice. On board, they had steam heating and even classrooms and libraries for the seafarers. In 1818, the British naval officer John Ross had charted part of the route; now everyone was sure that Franklin would discover the rest of it.

In July 1845, the crews of two whaling ships met the expedition in Baffin Bay, west of Greenland. They found Franklin in good spirits and confident of success. Then the *Erebus*, the *Terror* and 129 men disappeared into a maze of frozen islands. There was no further news from them. At the end of 1847, worried Admiralty officials organized search parties, and soon a dozen ships were hunting for Franklin. In 1850, searchers found the first traces of the missing expedition - graves on Beechey Island. Three of Franklin's men had died there during the winter of 1845-46.

Over 40 attempts were made to find Franklin and his men. Eventually, it was discovered that they had all perished.

Left Franklin's ships, *Erebus* and *Terror*, pick their way through the freezing waters of the Arctic in northern Canada in the summer of 1846. In the winter that followed, their way was blocked by ice, and the men soon fell prey to the harsh conditions. Many of them died within a few weeks, although Franklin survived until June 1847.

The Inuit of the Arctic used dog-drawn sledges for transport. When Franklin's ships were stopped by pack-ice, he and his men had to try to walk across the frozen landscape to safety.

Surrounded by the bodies of his dead crewman, Franklin prepares to die.

How did they die?

Franklin's men died of cold, starvation and scurvy when their food supplies ran out. Some may have developed lead poisoning from the primitive cans they took with them containing tinned meat. This would have made them confused and despairing.

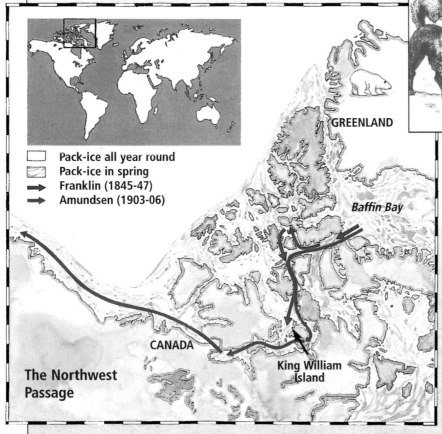

Pack-ice all year round
Pack-ice in spring
Franklin (1845-47)
Amundsen (1903-06)

GREENLAND

Baffin Bay

CANADA

King William Island

The Northwest Passage

Above One of the search parties sent to find Franklin was led by Leopold McClintock. Inuit hunters gave him proof of the fate of Franklin and his men.

Sadly, Franklin's men never learnt Inuit survival techniques, such as wearing furs to keep warm or building igloos for shelter. They encountered Inuit hunters on several occasions, but the Inuit were terrified by their wild appearance, and were even shot at by the ill-fated explorers.

Above The Northwest Passage was first navigated by the Norwegian Roald Amundsen in 1903-06.

So close to glory

If Franklin had sailed to the east of King William Island he would have escaped the ice and found the last uncharted stretch of the sea route. As it was, his mission was completed by his exhausted and desperate men as they marched to their death.

They found the last link in the Northwest Passage, but for them it was too late.

The aim in searching for the Northwest Passage was to find a shortcut from Europe to Asia. But, because of the ice and the terrible Arctic climate, the route turned out to be unusable. Tragically, hundreds of people lost their lives finding out. Not surprisingly, this bleak and dangerous route has sometimes been called the Seafarers' Graveyard.

The Northeast Passage

As well as searching for the Northwest Passage, some European countries also sent out expeditions to find a Northeast Passage to Asia, around the north of Russia.

Willem Barents, a Dutch explorer, led three expeditions in the 1590s, but he could not get any further than the island of Novaya Zemlya before being forced back by the ice.

During the eighteenth and early nineteenth centuries, map-makers gathered enough evidence to show that the Northeast Passage did actually exist. The first person to sail through it was the Swedish explorer, Baron Nils Adolf Nordenskjöld. After sailing from Stockholm in Sweden, he set out from Tromsö in northern Norway in July 1878, sailed through the Barents, Kara and Laptev seas to the north of Russia, and emerged through the Bering Strait a year later.

This map shows the route taken by Baron Nils Nordenskjöld (left) in his ship the *Vega*, on the first voyage through the Northeast Passage in 1878-79.

TIMELINE

c. 1490 BC

Hatshepsut of Egypt sends expedition to Punt

480 BC

Hanno of Carthage sails down west coast of Africa

310 BC

Pytheas sails to Thule

982

Erik the Red sails to Greenland

995

Leif Eriksson lands in Vinland

1405-33

Voyages of Cheng Ho

1488

Bartholomew Diaz rounds the Cape of Good Hope

1492-93

First voyage of Christopher Columbus to San Salvador and Hispaniola

1497-99

Voyage of Vasco da Gama to India

1498

Columbus reaches coast of South America

1499

Voyage of Amerigo Vespucci

1500

Pedro Alvarez Cabral claims Brazil for Portugal

1519-22

First voyage around the world, by Ferdinand Magellan and Sebastian del Cano

1606

Willem Jansz is first European to land on Australia

1610-11

Final Arctic voyage Henry Hudson

1642-44

Abel Tasman sails to Tasmania, New Zealand and along the north coast of Australia

1768-71

James Cook's first voyage, to Australia and the South Seas

1772-74

Cook's second voyage, around Antarctica

1776-79

Cook's final voyage, in search of the Northwest Passage

1845-47

John Franklin's expedition in search of the Northwest Passage

1878-79

Nils Nordenskjöld sails the Northeast Passage

1903-05

Roald Amundsen successfully navigates the Northwest Passage

GLOSSARY

Aborigines The first people to colonize Australia.

Admiralty The Department of the British Government that controlled the Royal Navy.

Astrolabe Navigational instrument designed to measure latitude by measuring the height of the sun.

Caravel A small coastal craft adapted and improved for exploring by Henry the Navigator.

Equator This is where an imaginary latitude line that runs around the middle of the globe. The equator is 0° latitude.

Great Barrier Reef A 2,000-km long series of coral reefs that runs along the eastern coast of Australia.

Inuit Native peoples of the Arctic coasts and islands of North America.

Kayak A seal skin covered canoe used by the Inuit.

Lateen Triangular type of sail that allowed the ship to take advantage of a side wind.

Latitude and longitude Imaginary lines used to find your position. Latitude runs West-East. Longitude runs North-South.

Magnetic Poles Points at the northern and southern ends of the earth's magnetic field.

Papyrus A type of water reed. The ancient Egyptians also used it to make a kind of paper.

Pilot On a ship the pilot is someone with a knowledge of a sea route who takes charge of steering the vessel.

Pole Star A star that appears to be above the north pole. As you go south the star appears to drop down towards the horizon.

Prow The pointed front end of a ship.

Rigging The ropes used to support the masts and work the sails of a ship.

Strait A narrow piece of water connecting two seas.

FURTHER INFORMATION

BOOKS

Buried in Ice by Owen Beattie and John Geiger (Hodder and Stoughton/Madison Press, 1992)

Ships and Shipwrecks by Steve Blackman (Watts, 1993)

Christopher Columbus by John D. Clare (Bodley Head, 1992)

The Usbourne Book of Explorers by Felicity Everett and Struan Reid (Usbourne, 1991)

Explorers and Discoverers by Neil Grant (BBC Fact Finders, 1992)

Medieval Map Makers by P.D.A Harvey (The British Library, 1991)

The Voyages of Captain Cook by Jason Hook (Wayland, 1990)

Ships Sailors and the Sea by Richard Humble (Franklin Watts, 1991)

Boat by Eric Kentley (Dorling Kindersley, 1992)

Explorer by Rupert Matthews (Dorling Kindersley, 1991)

The Brendan Voyage by Tim Severin (Hutchinson, 1976). This is one of a number of accounts of Severin's voyages in reconstructions of ancient ships. Although an adult book, it is accessible to children.

FILMS AND VIDEOS

The Norsemen (Rank Home Video) A Viking adventure about a prince who sails to North America to rescue his father from native Americans who have kidnapped him.

1492 The Conquest of Paradise (Guild Home Video) The story of Columbus and the effects of his voyages on the peoples of the Caribbean.

Mutiny on the Bounty (MGM) The story of the 1789 mutiny against Captain Bligh (who had earlier sailed with James Cook).

INDEX